Floating and Sinking

Sue Barraclough

Heinemann
LIBRARY

www.heinemann.co.uk/library
Visit our website to find out more information about **Heinemann Library** books.

To order:
☎ Phone 44 (0) 1865 888066
▤ Send a fax to 44 (0) 1865 314091
▢ Visit the Heinemann Bookshop at www.heinemann.co.uk/library to browse our
catalogue and order online.

First published in Great Britain by
Heinemann Library, Halley Court, Jordan Hill,
Oxford OX2 8EJ, part of Harcourt Education.
Heinemann is a registered trademark of Harcourt
Education Ltd.

Editorial: Dan Nunn and Stig Vatland
Design: Jo Hinton-Malivoire and Bigtop
Picture Research: Ruth Blair, Erica Newbery and
Kay Altwegg
Production: Duncan Gilbert

Originated by Chroma Graphics (Overseas) Pte. Ltd
Printed and bound in China by South China
Printing Company

10 digit ISBN 0 431 02425 1 (hardback)
13 digit ISBN 978 0 431 02425 7 (hardback)
11 10 09 08 07 06
10 9 8 7 6 5 4 3 2 1
10 digit ISBN 0 431 02430 8 (paperback)
13 digit ISBN 978 0 431 02430 1 (paperback)

11 10 09 08 07
10 9 8 7 6 5 4 3 2 1

British Library Cataloguing in Publication Data
Barraclough, Sue
  Floating and sinking. - (How do things move?)
  1.Floating bodies - Juvenile literature
  I.Title
  532.2'5
A full catalogue record for this book is available
from the British Library.

Acknowledgements
The publishers would like to thank the following
for permission to reproduce photographs:
Alamy pp. **6, 22 bottom** (Brand X Pictures), **11**
(Sarkis Images), **12** (RubberBall), **18, 23 top left**
(Dave Porter), **19, 23 top right** (Stephen Frink
Collection), **20, 22 top left** (Danita Delimont);
Corbis pp. **9** (Peter Barrett), **10, 22 top right**
(Ariel Skelley), **14** (Craig Lovell), **16, 17** (Rolf
Bruderer); Getty Images (Photodisc) pp. **7, 13, 21,
23 bottom**; Nature Picture Library p. **15** (Doc
White); Photolibrary p. **8** (Index Stock Imagery);
Punchstock p. **4, 5** (RF).

Cover photograph reproduced with permission of
Corbis (Stuart Westmorland).

Contents

Floating

If something stays on top of water, it **floats**.

These children are **floating** in a swimming pool.

Sinking

If something goes under water, it sinks.

These stones are **sinking**.

This boat has a hole. It is sinking too.

Helping you float

There are lots of things to help you **float** on water.

Floating fun

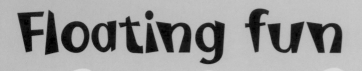

There are lots of ways to have fun **floating** on water.

Floating in a boat can be fun.
The air in this dinghy helps it to float.

Sinking fun

Swimming underwater can be fun too.

This diver has a special mask so she can stay underwater longer.

Animals in water

This sea otter can **float** on water.

It can dive down underwater too.

Skimming stones

Skimming stones is fun!

Plop!

Flat stones can bounce on water. Then they **sink** under the water.

Light and heavy

This beach ball filled with air is light. It **floats** on water.

What do you think?

This is a boat.

Do you think it will float or sink?

100358

This is a bicycle.

Do you think it will float or sink?

Floating or sinking?

Can you remember which things **float** and which things **sink**?

Index

Notes for adults

The *How Do Things Move?* series provides young children with a first opportunity to learn about motion. Each book encourages children to notice and ask questions about the types of movement they see around them. The following Early Learning Goals are relevant to the series:

Knowledge and understanding of the world
• Find out about and identify some features of living things and objects
• Ask questions about why things happen and how things work
• Show an interest in the world in which they live
• Encourage use of evaluative and comparative language

These books will also help children extend their vocabulary, as they will hear some new words. Since words are used in context in the book this should enable young children to gradually incorporate them into their own vocabulary.

Follow-up activities
• Ask your child to look around the house and identify three things that will float and three things that will sink. Then find out whether he or she is right by testing each item in a bowl of water together.
• Demonstrate how filling something with air can make it float by placing a blown-up balloon in a bowl of water alongside a balloon that has not been blown up. Ask your child to guess what is making the difference.